Daily Sentient
An Anthology of Emotion

E. P. Johnson

Dedicated to my roommates Celeste and Lexi,
who kept me sane and showered me in undeserved
kindness.
Thank you.

~ Note to the Reader ~

Dearest Listener,

Thank you for joining once again.
Welcome to the complexity of emotion. I hope to provide
an opportunity to dive deep into your emotions by diving
head first into mine. I encourage you to explore the
emotions you've been running from. However, I also
encourage you not read what you are not ready for. I
intended be as empathetic and honest as I could be. If
you read something you don't like, good. I hope not to
inflict hurt but instead to help you access yours.
This will be a painful read, proceed with grace and caution
for your heart.

I would like to start off by explaining that this book is a
direct testament of my faith and rejoice in God. Jesus
Christ is Lord and Savior over my life. I was brought to
God in 2014 when God showed me two dreams; heaven
and hell. I grew weary that God was truly listening and so I
prayed what I thought was going to be my last prayer. I
told God, if you're really so big and powerful then show
me where you live. I will now share with you those two
experiences.

~ Heaven ~

Forever upon us
Bewilderment sets in
Is this really eternity?
No senses
Total sensation
Lifting from my body
Flutters out
Weightless
Vibrance softens
The brightest my eyes have ever seen
No eyes
Heart enchanted
Surrounded
The love of the world
Everlasting
Purest silence
Expounds joy
Loved ones
From earth
From before
From after
Heavenly body inhabited
Awe
Unearned
Undeserved
Everlasting
Unconditional
Forever upon me
As it was in the beginning
So too in the end
God

~ Hell ~

Fear
I Fear
Where am I going?
What is that thing leading me?
Shadow
No answers
Confusion
The dread starts to well
The dread
Corners
Alleyways
Winding path
Treacherous
The moment of eternal truth
Evil burning
Smoldering of soul
Breaking the self to fit into a tiny hole
Nothingness
Why am I doing this?
Goodbye self
Goodbye goodness
Brokenness
Unsettled
Fear

It doesn't matter if you are religious, spiritual, non religious, or logically driven, everyone has emotions. In this book I have expressed mine. I do so from the perspective from which I feel them which often involves God. No two people experience emotions in the same way. I ask that in the midst of reading mine that you think deeply about yours.

This is my daily sentient.

Lovingly,
E. P. Johnson

~ Emotions ~

Part 1: Healthy
Happiness
Sadness
Anger
Love
Grief

Part 2: Destructive
Nostalgia
Loneliness
Despair
Emptiness
Numb

Part 3: Transcendent
Faith
Grace
Mercy
Lust
Curiosity

~ Part 1 ~

Healthy

~ Happiness ~

I am the bird
Covered in the oil of the spill
Flying high
Fighting the weight of my wings
Desperately flying at the sun
To see if it could have mercy on me
And melt the oily burden from my back
And the warmth of the sun
Warmed my heart
It reminded me that I am a part of the sun
And I am beautiful in creation
Burden or no burden
Life is beyond my heavy wings

~ Happiness ~

I saw your face in the moon today
It was a crescent and it was smirking at me
I dream so earnestly for the day your smirk is mine
I wonder if you'll ever feel as immensely as I feel for you
But more so I hope you have the guts to love
I want to see your smirk every day
For now
The moon will suffice

~ Happiness ~

Happiness is fleeting, fluttering
Like a butterfly
Only to land on you for a moment
Before deciding to fly away
I wonder where it's going
Who gets to keep it as a pet
But I don't want to keep it
It's meant to go beyond me
Float on its merry way
Only to bless me for moments at a time
Fleeting, fluttering

~ Happiness ~

Happiness is only beautiful
When it's mundane
It's the little moments
When you catch yourself smiling without reason
When gratitude drips from you like sweat
And you catch your breath for a moment

~ Happiness ~

You shall despair no more
Saith the Lord unto me
Hope shall win
All the days of your life

~ Happiness~

My acne?
I love them
They're part of what makes me ugly
And the ugly is what makes me beautiful
The sky is covered in stars
And isn't she beautiful
Just like me

~ Sadness ~

I am the bird
Covered in the oil of the spill
Flying high
Fighting the weight of my wings
Desperately flying at the sun
To see if it could have mercy on me
And melt the oily burden from my back
The sun never comes
The moon can't warm me like the sun can
And I grow tired in the night
The oil covers my eyes
Blind
Falling slowly backwards
I exhale what I pray is my last breath
To find myself stuck in the oil once more
Escapeless

~ Sadness ~

Hello sadness
I think I will always know you
The same way I will always know God
You and I will grow old together
Reflective with sorrow
Paging through my memories and inserting feelings of
nostalgia and regret
Thinking about times for which I was happy
And noticing the way you were always still there
I miss you when you're gone
But I resent you when you're near
Sadness you have treated me well
Given me a full range of experience
Maybe that's all I could ever want
Filled with gratitude even
Maybe

~ Sadness ~

I am my own magician
I will levitate myself out of my own depression
I will look at my emotions
From the safety of the cosmos
I will look down
And sort my emotions
In a manageable order
And swallow them one at a time
I will not pull a rabbit out of a hat
But I can make myself disappear
I won't do that anymore
Instead I will levitate
In and out of my realities
Until I am well

~ Sadness ~

Sadness sits in my thighs
My legs tingle and numb
As tears pour down my cheeks
I am unable to walk
I am unable to speak
But I'm releasing the feeling
Like unclenching a fist
Sadness manifests in my legs
Because it roots me
Moves me
Sadness is the anchor
For which I hold onto in the emotional storm
My mouth gapes like a fish
And I drown in the ocean of my tears
Sadness is my emotion
But also the wave I choose to ride
Woah is the wave
Woah is my tears
Yet I still stand
Sad but standing
Sad but standing

~ Sadness ~

Eternal sadness
An ethereal experience
One gets to float lightly above existence
And look down
And so authentically feel
The travesty of the human experience
Let in the true short nature of life
Allow the gravity of loss to weigh on the heart
Access the true suffering of the world
Weeping deeply
Softly suffering
An eternity of authenticity
Separate from identity

~ Sadness ~

The pain sits on the front of my forehead
I don't feel joy
I don't want to
Why should I with all of the deep suffering of the world
Who am I to be happy in the midst of depravity and chaos
It throbs guilt and sadness into my soul
Poisons my heart
For this life of sorrow I live

~ Anger ~

I am the bird
Covered in the oil of the spill
Flying high
Fighting the weight of my wings
Desperately flying at the sun
To see if it could have mercy on me
And melt the oily burden from my back
With every flap of my wings
I remember my suffering
Rage stirring
I fly toward the ship that hurt me
Red in my eyes
Tears streaming
I see a man
Before I know what I've done
I peck out his eyes
And I don't feel better

~ Anger ~

God is wrestling my insides
Like He once wrestled Jacob
I don't want to show you mercy
Like He has once shown to me
I grow anxious
Wondering if I have the forgiveness
But I can't forgive you
Because I understand hurting me
If you don't know me
But you knew me most
And boy, did you hurt me
And you still hurt me
I am still stuck on you
I am still mad at you
Screw you!
Fuck you!
But I still need to forgive
You deserve mercy
I owe youme that

~ Anger ~

Happy people
Are great deniers
They deny their pain
Embrace their future
And turn blind to their past
Hunt for the good in the bad
And live a life of lies
How dare they?

~ Anger ~

I want to burst
I'm so angry
I'm so frustrated
I hate everything
I hate the tears streaming down my face
I want to shove them back into my eyes
I hate that I can't focus
Everyone needs something from me
And I can't even give what I need to myself
I am so angry
I am so frustrated
I am so aggressive
I am so lonely
I am so isolated
Yet surrounded by people

~ Love ~

I am the bird
Covered in the oil of the spill
Flying high
Fighting the weight of my wings
Desperately flying at the sun
To see if it could have mercy on me
And melt the oily burden from my back
I fly so high
That I see the heavens
And I remember that I am so small
God is so big
My body isn't safe
But my heart has always been home to Something greater

~ Love ~

Tonight our souls connected
You can try to deny it
But I saw right through you
And you were scared
Our generation is fearful
Not just of being loved
But more so that they're incapable of returning it
Do not fear
My love is unconditional
I will love you even if you can't love me back

~ Love ~

I want to nestle my face
In the crook of your neck
I want to smell your skin
And dance cheek to cheek
Run your index finger
Down my spine
You are so special
To me
My soul is filled with love
And filled with me
You silence my worry
And turn off the light of loneliness
My beloved
Please don't hurt me
Because I can love you unconditionally
If you choose to be kind
I'll never ask you to love me
But I'll beg until I die

~ Love ~

I loved you so much
There was no use in asking for it back
I got such deep gladness
From my ability to love you
Despite knowing that you would never love me
I don't need to love again
I did it
I loved you so much that I watched you grow
Flourish
And dazzle
It invigorated me to know
What my love could do for you
I don't ever need to be loved
The way I love you
God's love
And my love
Surprise me
And delight me daily
My love taught me what I knew all along

That all the love I would ever need
Was already inside of me

~ Love ~

Love is fickle
You should marry the one you need
Not the one you want
But the one you want is the one you already chose to love
The one that slipped through your fingertips
The one who said that you were just too different and that
it couldn't work
The one who catches your eye in any room
The one that still chases you in your dreams
The one you will never wake up next to
The one who will is
Kind, sweet, safe, supportive
And just as deeply flawed as you
You owe them a great deal
They make you coffee
Ask you how your day was
Kiss you on the forehead
And stay up late to wash the dishes because you made
dinner
And they will never be the apple of your eye
The object of your desire
The one whose name wakes the dusty butterflies in your
stomach
You desire the stability and longevity of the one you need
But your heart will always belong to the one you want
Forever trapped in the dance of personal misery
Desire ruined the only thing good about life
Love
Because I will never truly love the one I truly need

~ Love ~

The love of God grows
It lingers in my soul
It delights and enchants
My joy is in His grace and mercy
He is close to my broken heart
And in my deepest sadness
He is with me
His loving hand
Holds my face and says
You are mine own child
My beloved
And for that moment
I know Love

~ Love ~

Love will always despair our connection
We can't be friends because we might want more
But we will always want more
So we will never be in love
Love wants for nothing
Love gives with an open hand
Expecting nothing more
I tried to love and succeeded
But I failed not
Let selfishness make my heart bleed
The poison of my desire for you ruins my love for you
Trap me in a passing train
And let me watch you go
Gripping only the future
Loving you only to let go

~ Grief ~

I am the bird
Covered in the oil of the spill
Flying high
Fighting the weight of my wings
Desperately flying at the sun
To see if it could have mercy on me
And melt the oily burden from my back
As I look down
I watch my loved ones covered in the oil
I cry so hard for them to come with me
To live
But they are dying
The oil covers their nose
It covers their mouth
I watch them choke
As I soar away
They are dying
And I am surviving

~ Grief ~

Today I remembered that you too would die
I became overwhelmed as tears shot of eyes before the
sorrow could even catch up
How I'm going to miss you
And how painful it will be to see you go
I grieve everyday for all those we've already lost
My heart is heavy with all the whom I will have to part with
soon

~ Grief ~

Holding your lifeless body
Your head rests on my chest
As I lay on my back
Run my fingers through your hair

Everything reminds me that you're gone
When I lost you, I felt as though
I lost him too
I miss you both
I miss your physical presence
I miss the way he used to be
Why couldn't you have been alive
Long enough to teach him how to be good
Why can't you still be around
Why did you choose to end it all?
Life has always been worth living
I don't know that it is now that you're gone
You got to release your pain
But you instead transferred it to us
I don't blame you
But you were so, so selfish
I miss you still
I miss you

~ Grief ~

I am so filled with grief
That if you nicked my skin
It would spill and pour all over
Even through a tiny cut
I scraped myself the other day
On a photo of you
And I bled so much
That no matter how much I smiled
No matter how much I bandanged it
It was evident it was boiling over
Sadness is the liquid
Fear is the fire
Held by a pot of dread

Grief make my skin crawl

~ Grief ~

Dearly Beloved,

We gather here today to mourn the loss of Emma's childlike happiness.
It lived a short life but it was a truly meaningful time. She laughed so much and was able to concern her small naive mind with the daily shortcomings and practicalities in life. Her vivaciousness and festiveness will be truly missed.

Not to speak ill of the dead but her childlike happiness held her back. It was something that kept her from truly seeing the world for what it was. When happiness was at the center of her life, God was not. Now that happiness is seperate from her, she can experience many deeper positive emotions like joy and gratitude.

She will always have a special place in her heart for happiness. Happiness was her partner in life and like a childhood best friend that eventually moved away. She will always miss you but she doesn't need you anymore.

Rest in Joy.

~ Grief ~

The scream
Is the exhale of the soul
And the only known cure for grief
A sign of release
Loving and piercing
Yell and shout
But only for yourself
Never for anyone else
Scream at God
Scream for God
Scream inside
Scream out loud
Scream for yourself
The scream

~ Part 2 ~

Destructive

~ Nostalgia ~

I am the bird
Covered in the oil of the spill
Flying high
Fighting the weight of my wings
Desperately flying at the sun
To see if it could have mercy on me
And melt the oily burden from my back
Tears in my eyes
I am consumed with longing
For the days that I was free
Free of the oil
Free of the torment
When my life was naive
When I was charmed

~ Nostalgia ~

To a high schooler,

I look at you with heavy eyes and a jealous heart. What I wouldn't give to go back to being 18 and carefree. I want to go back to the place you're in now. Just so I could experience being young and be conscious that I was young.

God I was so happy when I was your age. I thought I knew what I wanted to be when I got out of college, or what I wanted to be when I grew up. I thought I wanted to be my age and to be an adult have a real job and start my life already. I was wrong.

I wish I could shake you awake and tell you that you're young and broke and perfect.

You will never get this time back. Take it from someone who is now 21 and watching their youth fade into the abyss, being an adult is scary. When you're young, you know what love is and people are nice to you; even if it's only to get into your pants.

After two horrifying breakups and 5 deaths in three years all I can say is hold on while you're still young. Enjoy these fleeting moments with your friends before they all go to college and forget that you ever existed.

When you're 18 you know what love is. Hold onto this definition of love because I promise it exists.

Don't let anyone talk you out of this hopeful definition of true romantic love because it's the only thing worth living for. The adults who will try to talk you out of feeling that strongly for someone have all been divorced and never married the person they really loved.

This letter is bleak but it's not misguided. Cherish your time at this age because you'll never be as beautiful as you are in this moment. Love freely and live honestly.

And don't forget that things don't get better; that's a lie adults will tell you again and again. But things do change. They change for the better and the worse. The change is what makes it all worth it. Trust me, you'll want to be around when it all changes again.

Painfully,
nostalgia

~ Nostalgia ~

Scraped knees
Acne face
Teenagers never
Forget your place
Please get angry
Please get mad
Tell us adults
The pain you have
Pain on your heart
Pain on your face
I don't fit in!
I don't know my place!
Maybe I don't want to!
I'm a disgrace!
Get more angry
Maybe even sad
These times are fleeting
So good and so bad

~ Nostalgia ~

I miss your big sad puppy dog eyes
I miss the way they look up at me
I miss the way your eyelashes wag in my presence
I miss the way you always want to hear what I have to say
I miss you
I miss the time we spent together
And I regret that we didn't spend more
And I regret not telling you sooner
And I regret falling in love with you in three days
And I regret admitting that aloud
And I regret

~ Nostalgia ~

I was once a sweet girl
Bittered by my experiences
Soured by my suffering
Now that so many have died
I must be content spending my remaining days amongst
strangers
Who shall I be?
Where shall I dwell?
A restless soul captured by a jaded body
I have nowhere to lay my head on earth
Nowhere is safe
Everyone I come across
Wants to use my body for something
My soul can't bear it anymore
Lord take my body
My soul cries out for you now
Let me rest my being in your Loving Spirit
I am young
But I am settled
I am ready to go home Lord
Home to your Kingdom
My earthly body lay waste to the people
Who traumatized me
My hope lies in You, Lord
You alone
So I beg of you God
Make of flesh this heart of stone

~ Loneliness ~

I am the bird
Covered in the oil of the spill
Flying high
Fighting the weight of my wings
Desperately flying at the sun
To see if it could have mercy on me
And melt the oily burden from my back
And I fly to my freedom
I see the flock dying below
I cannot save them
I could only save me
Only forward
Alone

~ Loneliness ~

Oh God if you only knew
How this broken heart
Still beats for you

~ Loneliness ~

As the sun goes down
And moon finally glimmers
Your face melts into sunset
And drips deep into my heart
Your love
Is my favorite distant memory
Your crush a sweet, sticky delusion
Dripping down my hands
I want to share this imaginary love
With the world
Kiss me in my dreams
Kiss me in my nightmares
I want you for better
And for worse

~ Loneliness ~

Physical touch is the loneliest love language to have
You can ask your friends for gifts
You can ask your friends for service
You can ask your friends for words of affection
You can ask your friends for quality time

You cannot ask your friends
To kiss your lips
To lay in your bed
To hold your hand
To bite your fingers
To hold your gaze into the night
To run their nose and lips along your neck
Or to bite your thighs

So you have to wait for your lover to satiate you
Ravage your body
And delight your soul

~ Loneliness ~

How I envy you optimism
I covet your gift for joy
That God has not blessed me with
God has isolated me with my spiritual gift of wisdom
And as I envy you
I pity you all the same
I able to understand things you are not able to
I can see and feel things that you can't
People love and need me in crisis
You will want them to need you so bad
But in times of need, I'm needed
But they like to be in your company most
I am the pain and hurting
You are the joy and peace
I can show them truth
You can show them love
How treacherous and delightful a gift
I must learn to love my gifts as you have learned to love
yours
Until then
I will covet after joy
Slip deep into misery
And give light to truth and wisdom

~ Loneliness ~

Longing
Acceptance
Tears streaming
Face smiling
Missing
Yet complete
Joy
Sorrow
Nostalgia
The wind blowing the trees
As their leaves fall
Letting go of your hand
Looking up
Realizing you're better for my love for you
Realizing you're better because I let you go
Walking away

~ Loneliness ~

I've never wanted to be loved
I just wanted to be seen
I wanted someone to see my soul
But not to adore it

~ Despair ~

I am the bird
Covered in the oil of the spill
Flying high
Fighting the weight of my wings
Desperately flying at the sun
To see if it could have mercy on me
And melt the oily burden from my back
But I fly too close
And my wings set fire
And ablaze I am the boldest bird
More beautiful than my fellow flock
And as my ashes fall away
My spirit rises
I lose myself in freedom

~ Despair ~

I fear not death
I fear not life
I fear only living
To love is to live
And I lay shaking
Clinging to the cliff
Unwilling to fall again
In love with the fall
Contempt for the landing
Being heartbroken again is so unbearable
That I make have paralyzed myself for good
Knuckles bleeding
Teeth clenched
Running from love

~ Despair ~

Look at this pool of blood
It glistens in the moonlight
And frightens in the daylight
It is my body
I've imploded from the inside out
I am nothing but my insides
For I am inside out

~ Despair ~

Hello despair
Hello sentient darkness
Are you ready to join again?
Let's dive deep into emptiness
Down the black hole I fall
The devil holds my hand and guides me down
Why haven't You decided I was done, God?
Why do you take me to this terrible place again?
What from hell am I supposed to learn this time?
You have shown me darkness and mercy
Are you making bets with the devil again?
You've done nothing but test my heart and my brain
So I give up God
I will succumb to the darkness and I'm not coming back
this time

~ Despair ~

What do you love about yourself?
Honestly, I don't
I don't love who I am
I don't even like who I am
I'm a mess
I'm reactive, not interactive
I'm honest but not in the way people want me to be
I'm riddled with fear
Doubt
And hopelessness
I can't cope
I can't think
I only ever feel
I'm a slave to my emotions
I don't want to be me
But I don't know how to change
Most of who I am is unable to change
And who I am is deeply unworthy
Unworthy for God's work
Unworthy of love

~ Despair ~

It's lonely nights like these
When I forget why we're not together
I forget that we're incompatible
I forget that I can't stand you
I'm still in love with you
My lips still quiver for your neck
I just know if you ever called me again
I wouldn't be able to decline
If you had looked back
Even once
You would have met my eager eyes

~ Despair ~

The sun rises
The clouds quickly shuffle in to cover her morning joy
I look up
My fragile heart cracks
My muscles tighten
The tears pour from my eyes
And I miss the people who hurt me

~ Despair ~

The world is not hopeless
Rather I am hopeless
In the world

~ Emptiness ~

I am the bird
Covered in the oil of the spill
Flying high
Fighting the weight of my wings
Desperately flying at the sun
To see if it could have mercy on me
And melt the oily burden from my back
I grow sick
Sick with fear
Sick of myself
I vomit my insides
Purging any semblance of my old life
Nothingness
Flying into the fire of day
Soaring through the black of night
Losing myself
In the flight

~ Emptiness ~

Unworthiness
Cuts deep into my heart
And tells me lies
Whispers to the ghosts of my fears
Who tease me at night
Unworthiness
Delights in my despair
Prays that I stay lonely and afraid
Bites my nails more me
Sits on my chest so I can't breathe
Watches my happiness unravel
Unworthiness
Plants seeds of distrust for my Savior
Reminds me of my human fragility
Makes me feel tiny and insignificant
Stokes the fire of distraught
Ravages my deepest dreams

~ Emptiness ~

The deepest cavern in my heart
A truly God-sized hole
Has been stuffed with everything
Except the love of my Savior
I tried filling it with love
But I filled with lust
I confused the two for so long

All I ever needed was His love
Not his love

~ Emptiness ~

I got my heart broken
By someone who didn't love me
And I let it make my heart cold and bitter
Frozen in time
This hurt I bear
Has damaged my little beating heart
It flutters sporadically
For the ones I've loved
Who didn't love me back
And it makes my heart cold
All the days of my life
My beating empty heart
A shell made of broken glass
Once filled with the love I had
For men who didn't love me
And made my heart frigid
Barely beating
An empty shell
I remain
Empty

~ Emptiness ~

I am the hurting
I am the pain
I am the river
I am the rain
Pouring down my face
Pouring down my body
An aching of heart
It disintegrates, it's rotting
Into little pieces
I give myself away
Now I want it back
An empty shell I lay
What is there left!
I cry myself awake
Dreams are ever haunting
I'm drowning in my lake
Consciousness like a moment
I'm simply floating down
Who will I become next?
My mirror greets me, hollow frown

~ Emptiness ~

Dear God
Did I miss my only chance at love?
Was my fleeting soulmate my only?
Will I ever open up again?
Will I ever have the courage to love like that again?
Or is my best chance at love simply loving only You?
My weary soul has grown old
My beating heart closed up shop
Let my hollow chest be my only misery
For I can bear no more
Amen

~ Emptiness ~

I only miss you
Because I have no one else
Waiting for better

~ Emptiness ~

My heart is overwhelmed
Brimming with regret
Weighted like an anvil
With no safety net
I look at you and hear
The cries of your despair
But I have always been empty
It's more than I can bear
Please just walk away
So I don't have to first
All of me is hurting
Goodbye

~ Numb ~

I am the bird
Covered in the oil of the spill
Flying high
Fighting the weight of my wings
Desperately flying at the sun
To see if it could have mercy on me
And melt the oily burden from my back
There was no mercy
Covered in oil I remained
But I didn't care
I didn't wonder why

~ Numb ~

Tears well up
My brow furls the sail of sadness
Bottom lip curls
The lump in my throat grows
My heart beats slower
Blood pumps to my face
I'm ready to cry and
I can't
You stop me
The numbness in my heart
Like a blanket of fear
Draped over emotional expression
All I want to is feel sadness' warm embrace
Exchange a sloppy kiss with my ex-lover depression
Hold the hand of despair
And you stop me
You whisper
Not now

~ Numb ~

I don't want to be here
I don't want to be there
I don't like it here
But I don't know if I can get to there
Here is not good
But there might be worse
If I make it there
I might wish that I were here
I want neither
I want to crawl into a ball
And become a blob
Float around for a while
And then float away
Never being here or there
Never being anywhere

~ Numb ~

Pobreza
You fell in love
With the woman
I thought I could be

~ Numb ~

When you give your heart away too early
Their arms will always feel familiar
I know I shouldn't
And I definitely won't
But when I feel alone
I want to fall into you all over again
Hold me again
Like you used to
Like you never hurt me

~ Numb ~

As we sat in the car
Watching the city go by
I thought that if you had stabbed me
I wouldn't have noticed
I look in the mirror
And I see nothing
If I looked up
And saw eyes
With no face
I would feel nothing
I held your hand
And felt lifeless

~ Part 3 ~

Transcendent

~ Faith ~

I am the bird
Covered in the oil of the spill
Flying high
Fighting the weight of my wings
Desperately flying at the sun
To see if it could have mercy on me
And melt the oily burden from my back
And my wish is granted
I fly years and years
Earnestly waiting
And slowly
The more I grow steadfast in belief I will be free
The freer I become

~ Faith ~

I knew today would be great
The moment I scraped my knee
The blood I shed was painless
The ego I bruised was throbbing
God was humbling me
To prepare me to live graciously today
To correct my pride and prepare my heart
All this pain that comes
Is a flare shooting at a positive future
Thank you God
You've taught me humility and gratitude
So that all bad things may be made great in Your glory

~ Faith ~

Today I swallowed the moon
I absorbed her power
I am below God
Yet above the earth
I am neither godly nor human
I am lunar and floating
Soaring into the horizon of my present
Leaving both past and future behind
Letting the sovereign hand of God glide my body
And the moon light my path
I'm so humble
So vulnerable
So surrendered
And so secure

~ Faith ~

The best place to be is somewhere else
Oh Lord!
May my wandering soul never settle while I'm here on
earth

~ Faith ~

I have faith in two things and two things only
I have faith in God
And my own suffering

I trust in these two things whole-heartedly
I am ready to live a life of humbling servanthood
And to live out my quiet, sad, and twisted musings
Feeling everyday both renewed in God
And completely broken in body
God is so close to the brokenhearted
But this little soul is torn up and worn out
She begs for the mercy of her Savior
And cries for the mercy of her emotion
In torment she will live
Until she finally has the refuge of her Savior
For eternity

~ Faith ~

God is ripping away my identity from me
My body is ripping in half
I always thought I knew myself but suddenly I don't
Everything hurts because of it
It's embarrassing
The one person I'm supposed to know has become a
stranger

~ Grace ~

I am the bird
Covered in the oil of the spill
Flying high
Fighting the weight of my wings
Desperately flying at the sun
To see if it could have mercy on me
And melt the oily burden from my back
I looked toward God
A plea
But the oily burden was forgiven
It was always forgiven
The next burden was forgiven
I was forgiven

~ Grace ~

I dreamt that I was in painful prayer at the beach
My knees were tucked
My face pressed deep into the sand
My cry was muffled
My palms were face up
And bleeding
Bleeding love
Bleeding mercy
Bleeding pain
Bleeding surrender
I surrendered myself to You again
As I got sand in my eye lashes when my tears hit the sand
My sorrows as a wave I'm always riding
Sliding down my cheeks
Waiting for an answer

~ Grace ~

My face was torn in half
Before the Lord
Jesus took my left half
And death took the right
My hands were given to the Devil
And my feet were given back to the Lord
My faceless broken body
Like a Greek statue
Floating through time
A ruin

~ Grace ~

God is like syrup
Dripping down my hands
Dripping down my face
Oh Lord hallelujah!
How you cover me in grace
Your love is sticky
Soft and heavy
Difficult to contain
Easy to share with others
Always sweet
Always loving
You are my best friend
You really get me
Emmanuel!
Emmanuel!

~ Grace ~

True grace
Is the most powerful being in the world
Taking the time to hold me at night
Wiping tears from my cheeks
Carrying the bags under my eyes
And holding my hand when there 7 billion others who
need him just as badly

And then I betray Him
And He still loves me
In fact so much that His arms greet me with mercy
And shower me in love
When I deserve wrath and spite

Amazing grace

~ Grace ~

The serenity of the water
Beckons my eye
Suades my ear
She tells me of a gratitude
So deep and lovely
That my heart will never grow weary again
The gratitude for short simple life
And so I look again to the ocean
And she smiles back

~ Mercy ~

I am the bird
Covered in the oil of the spill
Flying high
Fighting the weight of my wings
Desperately flying at the sun
To see if it could have mercy on me
And melt the oily burden from my back
Flying high
The sun shone down
And melted all away
So I took a piece of the sun in my beak
And brought it to the birds still covered in oil
Sharing
The Son that saved me

~ Mercy ~

The rain is gone
And the sun is out
And I've had the best mental health I've had since I was
starting high school
I've had an emotionally honest summer
I've learned a lot
I published my first book
I am in a healthy place in my relationships with my family
I am in meaningful friendships with some truly wonderful
people
I've even somehow been treated nicely by men I've dated
this summer
Dare I say even respected?
I am not feeding into my despair
I am in good health and love the way I look
I am happier than I've felt in a long time
And I feel so unworthy
A deep aching unworthiness
I feel not just unworthy of ever being romantically loved
But I feel unworthy of the love of the relentless love of my
Savior
I don't believe I have ever been worthy of love
Or that I ever will be

~ Mercy ~

Do you know yet that I was made to disappoint?
I am riddled with sin
Set me free from my pedestal
For I am half above
And half below the earth
Heathen split by disgrace
Fighting my invisible battle
Let me be the infallible one that I am

~ Mercy ~

The sovereign hand of God chokes me out
He slaps me across the face
Some can learn from a stern shake of His fist
Or a loving pat on the head
But not I
I needed to be humbled so deeply
And so daily
That I can feel God's hand on my throat each day waiting
to correct me
But also God's hand holding mine to comfort me
I am afraid
But in the most loving Hands

~ Mercy ~

The scorn of thine own heart
Beats voraciously
As approaching mine own eye
I see her presence in yours
Gracious am I to have been saved by God
When I pass such a sight
Otherwise I would find myself so angry
That I might lay a punch on your timid face
Her I blame not
You I blame deeply, myself I blame too
And despite these truths
Seek me out, you do
Oblige my requests, you have never
And never shall you
I cannot expect you to and so in my broken heart's
defense
I choose no expectations
Still I bleed with mine own love for you
From a scorned and damaged heart
A choice I made long ago
That has still yet to relent
Release me from my despair
Seek me out no longer
Have mercy

~ Mercy ~

As I let God's loving spirit into the depths of my heart
I found her
The despair
Taking shelter
In the last hole in my heart
Left by my own feelings of unworthiness
A hole burning and yearning to be filled with God's
everlasting love
God had been waiting for me to discover it all along
The despair would go away
The day I stopped feeding her
With a God sized chasm
God now
My heart is Yours
Tetelestai

~ Lust ~

I am the bird
Covered in the oil of the spill
Flying high
Fighting the weight of my wings
Desperately flying at the sun
To see if it could have mercy on me
And melt the oily burden from my back
As I flew higher
I looked below
The dark black oil shone in the sun
Glimmering
It was so gorgeous
That I fell right back in
And got stuck

~ Lust ~

I bury my whole self in my coping mechanisms
I can never just try one out
I dive deep
I either dive deep into the rush of male attention and lust
Or I dive deep into the Christian religion
Or both which is when I hate myself the most
Lord have mercy on that dark place of self loathing
How do I just dive deep into God and sacred sexuality?
Someone please teach me how to do this

~ Lust ~

I love you
And I don't know how to tell you
How do you feel about me?
Because I yearn for your attention
It doesn't matter
I chose you
I just have to wait
We will have a long love story
I will just have to be patient enough to see it through
How do I even say it?
I swear I sound mad
But I see it
Spending my life with you
I don't know if I miss you
Or love you
Or both
But damn do I want you ever

~ Lust ~

I am the promiscuous woman
Wearing crop tops
And bralettes
And lacy things
To tease to eyes and hearts of men they say
They say that I am easy for sex
Because I have chosen to have it
I am the meek little prude
Don't touch me
Button that top button
I want to be married and settled someday they say
My life to be dictated by others
Opinion after opinion on what I choose to share
Do I share my love?
Do I share my vagina?
Do I share my dangerous eyes?
Do I share my temptation?
Or dare I share my brain?
Either way I shift back and forth
Do I want to be perceived as the good Christian woman?
Or just as a simple slut?

~ Lust ~

There's a part of my heart
That used to be filled
By sleeping with you
I tried packing it with other yous
But they are just as empty as our love
I had no commitment
And you had no love
I tried to fill it with God
But I'm okay with it remaining empty
The selfish heart remains empty
Waiting foolishly for the next soulmate
But you were the soulmate
You are the soulmate
The heart remains empty

~ Curiosity ~

I am the bird
Covered in the oil of the spill
Flying high
Fighting the weight of my wings
Desperately flying at the sun
To see if it could have mercy on me
And melt the oily burden from my back
When I was stuck below
I knew
I just knew
That there was something better
There had to be
Flying
Toward wonder

~ Curiosity ~

Our world will always be in argument between two people
Those who hold to control
Those who hold to release
It will always be a push and pull in all of us
Those two people within us never agree
And somehow guide all of our actions
Neither can exist without the other
Control is misery
But release is destruction
Who will I be?

~ Curiosity ~

I want to sit where you sit
I want to lay where you sleep
I want to hear the voices you hear
I want to love you better
I want to taste what you taste
I want to smell what you smell
I want to touch what you touch
I want to see you better
I want to feel what you feel
I want to think like you think
I want to dream what you dream
I want to know you better
Will you let me love you?
Will you let me see what you see?
Will you let me know you deeper?
Will you let me in?

~ Curiosity ~

Why have my emotions been so egregious to me?
What have I ever done to them
I desire to be kind to myself and my emotions run wild
Like a snake in the grass
They reach forth and grab
No contrite my heart doth bear
But in all honesty
What the fuck?
Who are my emotions to grab me by the throat
And strangle my consciousness dry?
Who am I allow them?
Who am I?

~ Curiosity ~

I look into tunnel
Searching for a light
My life alone in front of me
I feel it all constricting
Even though I am totally free
There is nothing before me
Nothing behind
So I clutch to His hand
And pick the road less traveled